# TOILET BOWL CHRISTIANITY

## PURGE YOUR PAST FOR A REDEMPTIVE FUTURE

# Ken Freeman

TOUCH
PUBLISHING

Published by Touch Publishing
P.O. Box 180303
Arlington, Texas 76096 U.S.A.
www.TouchPublishingServices.com
Edited by Kimberly Soesbee

Scripture quotations are taken from the Holy Bible, New Living Translation, copyright ©1996. Used by permission of Tyndale House Publishers, Inc., Wheaton, Illinois 60189.

1. Religion / Christian Life / Spiritual Growth
2. Religion / Christian Life / Devotional
17.08.01

Library of Congress Control Number:  2017950055

# DEDICATION

To Jeff McGowan, my John the Baptist. He was God's voice to me.

To my Jesus Parents, Malcolm and Johnnie. They gave me a home and a hope in the Holy Spirit.

To my righteous fox, Debbie, who has given me her love, support, prayers, and constant encouragement to serve Jesus.

To Castle Hills First Baptist Church and Jack Taylor. They gave me roots for my faith and showed me that greater is He that is in me than he that is in the world.

Especially to those who have grown up in a godly household, have been saved at an early age, who have never really wavered, and have held steadfast to the faith. This book goes out to you; it was birthed by you. If I could choose a testimony it would be yours. Don't ever be ashamed of your testimony.

Revelation 12:11

# ACKNOWLEDGEMENTS

Thanks to Alicia Gregg, without her help this book would have never been written.

Thanks to Debbie (babe) for your commitment to me and my ministry. Thanks for loaning me out to churches, camps, and conferences. You are a Proverbs 31 wife. Thank you for being an incredible mom and grandmother. I love how you serve the Lord in our neighborhood, with our family, and in our church. You have been a strength, an incredible helpmate, and my best friend serving Jesus.

Thanks to the pastors and churches who have allowed me to tell my story. Without you I wouldn't have a job.

Thanks to you, the reader. As you read may it give you boldness to tell your story to someone else.

And most of all, thanks to The Dude, Jesus Christ. Without Him I would be nothing.

Philippians 1:8

# TABLE OF CONTENTS

# FOREWARD

Ken had been part of the youth group at our church in Corpus Christi, Texas. When we heard that he was living in St. Louis with his mom and having lots of problems, we were familiar with what he was facing again. His mom was an alcoholic, and Ken had to deal with several husbands in her life. With no spiritual encouragement whatsoever, Ken had begun to slip into despair and several bad habits followed. I was the minister of music at Castle Hills First Baptist Church in San Antonio, Texas. God had been doing a marvelous work in our church in the early 1970s, and my wife and I felt that God wanted us to invite Ken to come live with us for a while and had no idea how we would manage with a teenager living with us. We did know one thing and that was that it was what God wanted us to do so He would work out the details.

It did not happen overnight, but gradually we saw God's hand changing Ken. He moved from a cowed down walk with hanging head and depressed personality to a young man filled with the love of Jesus—head high, shoulders back, a song in his heart and a passion to tell others about Jesus. I was not surprised that God called him into the ministry. He empathizes with teenagers in their valley of problems and knows what a dysfunctional family is all about. His heart goes out to the addicted and the afflicted because

Christ is in him revealing His love through Ken to others. Ken's story is God's story, seeking the lost lamb and longing for the prodigal to come home into the arms of God. Read this book and listen to the voice of God calling you. Give your life to Him and, like Ken, find a wonderful new life of love, security, acceptance, and joy in God's forever family.

In Christ,

Malcom and Johnie Grainger,
Ken's "Jesus parents"

# PREFACE: Spiritually Throwing Up

So there I was in Energy, Illinois. I had woken up in the middle of the night to immediately recognize the queasiness in my stomach. Though I tried to think happy thoughts of my wife, Lassie, Barney, or anything to get my mind off of the room that was spinning around me, I finally gave in and made my way quickly to the bathroom. It wasn't long before my head was hanging in the commode, and I was throwing up things that I'd eaten in the first grade. I was sweating, and my hands were shaking. I was miserable.

It was at that point that I came to the conclusion that my head was in a place... well, it was in a place where heads aren't supposed to be. I believe we should have two commodes, one for throwing up, the other for our other business.

As I crawled back into bed, I noticed that even though I didn't want to throw up, it did make me feel better. I began to get my color back, my temperature slowly went back to normal, and my stomach finally felt better.

Sharing our testimony is a lot like throwing up.

It's normally something we don't want to do, sometimes it can hurt, the process can be uncomfortable and even miserable; but after it's over, we feel much better. In both cases, there is something in our body that needs to come out. In one instance, it's the nachos I ate in the first grade; in the other, it's the testimony that God has given me. Throwing up can make us better physically, and throwing up our testimony can make us better spiritually.

In this book, I hope to lead you into a better understanding of the story that God has given you and to lead you to a point where you are ready to "throw up" (share your testimony) on all of your family, friends, co-workers, and even an occasional stranger. Learning to share your testimony and throw up God's truth in your life will lead you into a deeper and more intimate relationship with God, and I guarantee you'll feel a lot better afterward. Join me as I throw up the rest of my adventure and share with you a few pointers on throwing up yours.

# ANGER MANAGEMENT

I felt like I was in the movie *Anger Management* with Adam Sandler. As we sat in our seats, a security worker came to ask him to calm down. After a short, heated discussion, the security guard pulled out a stun gun to calm Sandler. Just like Sandler had a confrontation with the security guard, I once had a confrontation with God. (God didn't have to pull out the stun gun on me, though.)

"God, I don't want to share my testimony again!" I pleaded, as I sat disgusted with the thought of having to share my story even one more time. "Come on, I have another message ready. I can teach out of your Word, God. Please don't make me tell it, please!"

It was 2001, and I was in the midst of my sixth year of ministry with Wild Week Summer Camps. It was our last night at camp in Jacksonville, Florida, and there were hundreds of students ready to hear what they had waited for all week, my testimony. They were just dying for me to throw up all over them.

From day one of camp, and any other event, everyone always asks me the question, "What night are you going to give your testimony?" My answer is normally the same, with my testimony always falling on the last night of the camp or revival.

With this said, it was obvious my time had come at this particular camp to give my testimony. Unfortunately, I wasn't as ready to share my testimony as everyone else was to hear it. So as I pled with God, I had the band Among Thorns play through a few more songs. In fact, I think they may have played through every song they knew that night. I kept waiting to hear them play "Kumbaya," and I would take that as a sign that it was far past my time to be on stage.

As "Kumbaya" was drawing dangerously near, God spoke to me. His voice wasn't audible, but was still unmistakably clear, "Freeman," which is what God has always called me, "the strongest sermon you preach is your testimony."

I sat, just thinking about what God said to me, and I realized that His comment to me was true for all people. The most powerful message that anyone has is his testimony. Convinced, finally, that God did want me to share my testimony one more time, I knew that God had also shed new light on an old story. It was at this point that I decided to look up the word "testimony" in my Bible, and God led me to John 1:6:

*"God sent John the Baptist to tell everyone about the light so that everyone might believe because of his testimony."*

God used John the Baptist's testimony to convince people that Jesus was real. The same is still true today. Though many people believe they can argue with God's word and the Bible, no one can argue with what God has done in the lives of His children. This is why our testimony is so powerful; because it can't be argued by unbelievers.

Still wanting more, I found John 5:31-38:

*"If I were to testify on my own behalf, my testimony would not be valid. But someone else is also testifying about me, and I can assure you that everything he says about me is true. In fact, you sent messengers to listen to John the Baptist, and he preached the truth. But the best testimony about me is not from a man, though I have reminded you about John's testimony so you might be saved. John shone brightly for a while, and you benefited and rejoiced. But I have a greater witness than John—my teachings and my miracles. They have been assigned to me by the Father, and they testify that the Father has sent me. You have never heard his voice or seen him face to face, and you do not have his message in your hearts, because you do not believe in me—the one he sent to you."*

It is important to understand that during biblical times it was vital to have two witnesses, or two testimonies, regarding a matter. In these verses, in which Jesus is speaking, Christ declares Himself to have the ultimate testimony. Having two testimonies with the testimony of John the Baptist concerning Jesus and Christ's testimony regarding Himself, we are valid in knowing that God is who He says He is. The same is true for Christians today, with our testimony being validated by the testimony of the Spirit of God who bears witness for us, which led me to my next verse.

The verses in 1 John 5:6-12 show us that even the Spirit of God and God have testimonies. The Spirit of God testifies that Jesus is God's Son through His baptism in water and His shedding of blood on the cross, and God's testimony is that "He has given us eternal life, and this life is in his Son" (1 John 5:12). It's amazing that testimonies are so vital that the Trinity—God, Jesus, and the Holy Spirit—all found it important to bear testimony themselves. This shows us how important our testimony can be.

I knew at this point that I not only needed to go on stage and share my testimony with the students there, but I also needed to encourage them to go into the world and share theirs. Throughout my years in the ministry, I found that many people don't feel as if they have a testimony because their past is not littered as mine was; with abuse, drugs, alcohol, molestation, sex, and anger. Instead, some have grown up in Christian homes, were saved at a fairly young age, and for the most part have walked the straight and narrow their entire lives. I had to make sure these students left understanding that their testimony was just as important as mine, and far more unique.

So as I walked on stage, I began to share with the students the verses that I came across and the conversation that I shared with God. I asked the question, "How many of you, after hearing my testimony and realizing that you have never really smoked, cursed, been involved with alcohol, and you're still a virgin, feel as if you don't have much of a testimony or that your testimony isn't as powerful as mine?" Of the nearly eight hundred students that filled the auditorium that night, about two hundred students raised their hands, an unfortunate sign that my testimony had become the norm.

As I explained to these students that we all have testimonies, I asked another question, "How many of you, who raised your hand before, would trade your clean testimony for mine?" Not one of the students that had raised his hand previously showed any interest in having my testimony. At that response, I immediately explained that I would be more than willing to trade my testimony for theirs, and I had these students, who had felt as if they didn't have a testimony, stand up all around the auditorium.

One reason I believe students who have clean testimonies believe they don't have one is because they believe that theirs isn't shocking or interesting. When I share my testimony, I share that God saved me from hell, not only eternally, but he also saved me from the hell that was my past. From the world's point of view, I should be an alcoholic and drug abuser, a wife beater and a deadbeat, but it's true that God can use all things for His glory, which is why God took my past mess and made it His message. However, as time goes on, my message tends to be less shocking, and the message of those students who, for the most part, have lived clean, godly lives, are becoming more and more shocking. The response of the students that night in Florida was proof of that. My goal was to share that the testimonies of the students who have lived lives of good choices are even more powerful than mine.

"You see," I addressed the students, "people clap for me and recognize me all the time, and I've lived a pretty messed-up life, but I want you all to understand that all of our testimonies are powerful. Some of the most powerful are the testimonies of the students who feel as if they don't even have one." Those students who felt as if they had no story to tell received a standing ovation that night. I pray they'll remember that night and allow it to encourage them to push on toward the prize, keep their eyes on Jesus, and realize how important and powerful their testimony can be.

Recently, I received an e-mail from the grandmother of a young lady in Tyler, Texas. Maggie was a young teenager, only fourteen or fifteen, and came with her group to hear me speak several times. In the many times that she heard me speak, she became very familiar with my testimony. Maggie's testimony was much different than mine; she was saved young and for the most part, walked the straight and narrow her entire life. Later, I found out that Maggie, like the students in Florida, felt as if she didn't have much of a testimony either, and what I read in her grandmother's e-mail both shocked and saddened me.

Maggie, one Friday night, decided to go to a mall with a group of friends. Somehow she became separated from the girls she went with, and she was approached by a group of young men. Eventually, she was dragged behind the mall and raped by these men. Her grandmother asked that I call and talk to her. What she said during that phone call has stuck with me ever since: "Ken, now I have a testimony like yours."

Sadly, I believe Maggie's comment came from an attempt to try to look on the "bright" side of her situation. I really believe she felt that without that horrible event happening in her life she didn't have much of a testimony or shocking story to tell. The truth is, however, that the effectiveness of Maggie's testimony didn't change the night she was raped. Her testimony was always powerful and was changed in a situation she couldn't control.

Revelation 12:17 says, "Then the dragon," which is Satan, "became angry at the woman, and he declared war against the rest of her children—all who keep God's commandments and confess that they belong to

Jesus." (The New International Version reads, "holds to the testimony of Jesus.") The children referred to in this verse include everyone who has a testimony. This verse shows that Satan has declared war on the children of God, but when looking back at Revelation 12:11, Christians can rest assured that they have within them the weapon to defeat the enemy. "And they have defeated him because of the blood of the Lamb and because of their testimony." This verse is proof that our testimony, regardless of our story, is vitally important.

As Christians, God has equipped us all with a story, or testimony, to tell. I've heard many people describe their "testimony" as "I've been baptized," or, "I'm a good person," but being a good person or being baptized does not mean that we have accepted Christ's free gift of salvation. For those of you whose story sounds similar to these, you may search through your past and ask yourself when you really accepted Christ as your savior. Also, for those who can define a moment of salvation, understand that your testimony isn't just the story of how you got saved. Your testimony encompasses your past, which brought you to the point of salvation, and the events in your life that happened after your salvation. Some of the events in our testimony may be events that are results of choices we have made, while others, like the event that changed Maggie's life, may remain far out of our control. Regardless, I know my testimony is forever growing and will continue to do so until Christ takes me home.

Finally, remember this: John the Baptist had a testimony (John 1:19-23). He was even accused of being the Messiah. I've only been accused of being the devil. John made himself a voice crying out in the wilderness. Be like John the Baptist, a voice that speaks out for Christ in your school, your work, and your home. Throw up on someone today.

Jesus also had a testimony. John the Baptist's testimony was his voice; Jesus' testimony was His life. Be the Jesus in your school, your work, and your home. Let your testimony not only be your words, but your life.

You do have a testimony! Make sure your testimony is pointing people toward Jesus, not turning them away.

## DEVO

Is there something God wants you to do right now that you are arguing with him about?

What is the first step you need to take in following what God would have you do?

Read Jonah 1-3:3.

Many times in our lives, God asks us to do something that we aren't crazy about doing. Just like Jonah, we have a choice. We can run from God or follow God. It's funny, as humans we truly believe we can run and hide from our maker. Adam and Eve hid in The Garden, and Jonah ran to hide from God in Jonah 1. Just as God found Adam, Eve, and Jonah, God finds us when we run from His will. God then continues to call us to the very task that we ran away from in the beginning.

Think of all Jonah had to endure because he didn't just follow God in the first place. Then, after enduring what he had, God still called him to Nineveh. How much easier would it have been for Jonah had he just followed God's will the first time?

## Challenge

Take ten minutes to pray. You get the first two minutes for talking. Ask God where He wants to use you. Spend the remainder of time allowing God to speak to you. Identify the first step you need to take to follow Him, and prepare to do so.

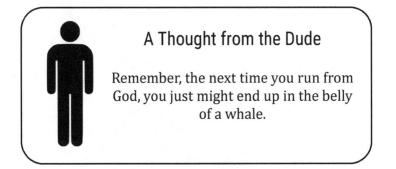

### A Thought from the Dude

Remember, the next time you run from God, you just might end up in the belly of a whale.

# THROWING UP THE TRUTH

For those of you who haven't heard my testimony, you probably don't understand why I find it so hard at times to stand before people and throw up my past. What happened that night in Jacksonville, Florida is not an uncommon event. However, it was the first time I ever argued with God about having to share my story because sharing my testimony has come to feel a lot like blowing chunks. It sounds gross, but it's reality. If He hasn't already, God, one day, will take you to that gross reality. Sometimes, however, we have to deal with the gross realities in our life. In fact, if we don't deal with them, they will deal with us.

This reminds me of an illustration I use when I share my testimony. Many of you have seen Disney's *The Lion King*. I remember a particular scene in the movie where the monkey, Rafiki, hit Simba on the head with a stick. Rafiki then tried to hit Simba again, but Simba ducked this time. The line that followed was a line of great theology, "You can run from your past, or you can learn from your past." Simba quickly learned that Rafiki was going to hit him with the stick, and because of this, Simba learned to duck. Just like Simba learned from his past, sometimes we have to learn from our past and refuse to let it define who we are.

I had nine step-fathers while I was growing up, not to mention the many other men who always came and went in and out of my mother's life. My biological father walked out of our lives when I was four years old, and my sister and I were left in East St. Louis with my mother and her terrifying addictions.

Mom was an alcoholic and was often involved with other drugs as well. (Alcohol is a drug.) Many times she brought her "fun" home with her, and wild parties took place frequently in our living room. When people came to our house it was only to pass out or party. Our lives were incredibly unpredictable. The only constant we could count on was the certainty of uncertainty, the promise of chaos.

Mom sometimes dropped off a bag of White Castle hamburgers and fries or Kentucky Fried Chicken for my sister and me on a Friday and didn't come home again until late Sunday night. Many times she came home completely drunk, and she verbally and physically abused my sister and me. I remember her cursing at us and telling us that we came from hell. There were many times that she hit us over and over again on the back of our legs with a broomstick. There were also times she threatened to kill us. My mom was always drunk; she woke up drunk, went to bed drunk,

18

and went to work drunk. I don't mean drunk with alcohol. You can be drunk with a lot of things. Lies. Lust. Deception. Fears. Worries. Bitterness. Unforgiveness. Hate. My mom was drunk with hate.

What are you drunk with?

I'll never forget the night mom came home from a long night of drinking and passed out in our kitchen. I remember being emotionally and physically exhausted, and as I stared over her lifeless body on the cold kitchen floor, all of the hate and anger for my mom began rushing through me. A butcher knife lay on the kitchen counter, and I remember running the blade of that knife up and down my mother's body as I sobbed and longed to kill her. I don't know if I chickened out or if God intervened, but I left my mother unharmed that night. For you see, I, too, was drunk. I was drunk with rejection and hate.

On another occasion, Mom left my sister and me with a babysitter, an ex-boyfriend of hers, while she went off for yet another drunken weekend. On the first night of her three-day absence, my mother's ex-boyfriend raped my five-year-old sister and molested me as a seven-year-old. Why? Because he too was drunk. He was drunk with perversion and lust.

Our location changed often, as I found myself in twenty-four different schools growing up, and five different high schools during my senior year alone. The abuse and neglect never stopped. At the age of nine, I attempted suicide, taking an entire bottle of aspirin before I went to bed. I don't think I wanted to die; I hink I just wanted the pain to stop.

As I grew up, I participated in many of the same activities I saw my mother participate in over the years. I took up alcohol as my drug of choice, as well as cigarettes on a daily basis. At one point I decided I had to get away, and I moved with one of my step-fathers to Corpus Christi, Texas.

It was in Corpus Christi where I met Jeff. Jeff was a football player and was also from a broken home. However, there was something different about Jeff's life that was very unlike mine. Jeff seemed happy. He had something that I didn't have. It wasn't long until I found out what that something was. Jeff was a member of a church, and he wanted me to join him for the ride. Jeff, too, was drunk. He was drunk with Jesus.

Finally, after Jeff's many attempts to get me to go with him, I gave in. After all, there was going to be free food and hot girls. I liked chicks and chicken.

As we walked into the church building, I followed Jeff all the way up to the choir loft where we found our seats. Yes, my first time at church I joined the youth choir! However as the night went on and the evangelist, Freddie Gage, preached, I felt God working on my heart, and by the time the night was over, I accepted Christ as my Savior and Lord of my life. I have never been the same since.

Shortly after my salvation, circumstances out of my control forced me to move back with my mother in St. Louis. However, I hadn't been there long when I received a phone call from Malcolm and Johnnie Grainger. They were a couple that I met at the church I attended when I lived in Corpus Christi, and they wanted me to come live with them in San Antonio. I call them my Jesus parents. They were the parents I always wanted, and they helped me in my walk with Christ.

As time went on, I found that there were several things I had to do to enhance my walk with Christ. One of these things was forgiving my biological parents for the abuse and neglect they put me through. This resulted in me placing phone calls to both my mother and my father to ask for their forgiveness. This included calling my father, who I hadn't seen or talked to in sixteen years. The phone call was short and ended as he hung up on me, and I didn't hear from my dad again for many years. My dad, too, was drunk. He was drunk with guilt.

In 1998, right before my first book was published, I met with my father for the first time since I was four years old. I was forty-six. The meeting almost never happened because my dad didn't know if he wanted to bring me back into his life again, but I waited patiently until finally I received a phone call from him saying that he was ready to see me. My wife, oldest son, and I packed up and flew to San Francisco, where he was currently living. The meeting was a little awkward, but we all cried and hugged and caught up on the years. I even had an opportunity to share the gospel with my dad, but he said he was too old to change his life.

Though there have been many ups and downs in life, my walk with Christ became my constant. In a world of chaos, Christ was my strength, and he has been ever since. God has blessed me so richly in this life. I have a beautiful wife who is my best friend and has stuck by me every step of the way, two sons whom I love dearly, and now several grandchildren who my wife and I love to spoil.

God led me into several years of youth ministry and eventually into full-time evangelism, which I'm still involved in to this day. You see, I should be a lot of things: a wife beater, an alcoholic, a thief, and a child abuser, but instead of running from my past, I decided to learn from my past. I chose not to allow my past to control my life, but to allow Christ to control my life instead, and that made all the difference.

One way that I deal with my past is by sharing it. Every time I share my testimony, I defeat all of the filth and evil that dwelled in my life before, and I ultimately get to concentrate on the glory and victory that God has given me through His Son, Jesus Christ. Now, I've become a magnet to youth and adults who find themselves in lifestyles or situations similar to mine. God allowed me to endure what I did as a child because

His purpose for my life included showing others who have similar lives that there is hope; there is a Person who can save them from the mess they are in and drastically transform their lives. If I didn't share my testimony, I would miss those opportunities to fulfill God's purpose. Just the other day, I heard this statement again, "I never knew that anyone knew how I felt." That's why I have to keep throwing up (sharing my testimony).

The same is true for you. Though some situations we find ourselves in are the results of bad choices we made in our past, some situations are the result of nothing we did. For example, my growing up in the environment I did had nothing to do with any choices I made. I was born into that situation. We all have situations that are outside of our control that become part of our testimonies. Regardless of what your testimony may be, God gave you that specific testimony for a reason. Whether you have a completely clean testimony or a wretchedly ugly testimony like mine, God wants you to share it with others.

John 9:1-3 tells the story of a blind man. The disciples asked Jesus if the man was blind because of his sins or the sins of his parents. Jesus' response was different from the thoughts of the time. Jesus said the man was blind because God planned to receive glory through his blindness. Sometimes we are born blind, disabled, abused, or neglected because it's God's way of receiving glory.

There is always a purpose in enduring the things life puts before us, and if we don't grasp that purpose of giving God glory, then enduring the situation was in vain. If I would have made the choice to never share my testimony, but rather chose to just reap the blessings of my new life in Christ, all that I endured in my childhood would have been in vain. The molestation, the abuse, the neglect, they all would have just been events that happened in my life that served no purpose but to traumatize me. However, because I choose to share my testimony with others, though it may be hard, I see that there was a purpose for those things happening to me. I can relate to another child who has been molested or abused. I can relate to an adult who is still bitter over his parents' divorce. Mostly, I can lead these individuals to the same hope and the same love that I found decades ago, Jesus Christ. All because I've learned to share my testimony. (I'm still throwing up.)

## DEVO

Is something in your past keeping you from God's best in your life?

How could God use that event in your past to lead others to him and enhance your testimony?

Read Acts 8:1–3 and Acts 9:1–31.

Paul had an incredible testimony. Known first as Saul, he made a choice to persecute Christians during the first part of his life. After Saul became a Christian, he suddenly had a past that he was not so proud of. However, rather than moping around about what he had been, he made the choice to validate the saving grace of Christ. God also used the fact that Saul was very well-known by the people to give him a voice to preach about the very thing that just days before, he persecuted.

God had an incredible plan for Saul's life. In fact, the life of Saul, or Paul, is still affecting us today. God said in Acts 9:15 that Saul was his chosen instrument to carry God's message. We see this message whenever we read Romans, 1 and 2 Corinthians, Galatians, Ephesians, Philippians, Colossians, 1 and 2 Thessalonians, 1 and 2 Timothy, and Titus, as Paul was a writer in all of these books. Despite Paul's past, God used his testimony in incredible ways. He longs to use yours in the same way. God has a purpose for all of us. What if Paul let the past hinder his future? The same is true for you.

## Challenge

We all have something lurking in our past that we aren't proud of. What is lurking in your past? Brainstorm ways that you can take control of that incident and move forward in your life. Maybe you need to place a phone call to apologize, maybe you need to work on forgiving yourself, or maybe you need to work on rebuilding a broken relationship. One way or another, take action. Do something that forces you to look your past straight in the face so you can take another step away from it.

## A Thought from the Dude

There's a time to throw up, and a time to take your head out of the commode.

# I BET YOU WOULD HAVE BEEN A GREAT SON

After seeing my dad for the first time in 1998, my family and I made it a priority to keep in touch with him following that meeting. We saw him only a few times since that first meet-up, but we regularly sent cards and letters and occasionally exchanged phone calls to keep in touch. Through those letters and phone calls I continued to tell him about what Christ was doing in my life. However, Dad believed that if you were a good enough member of the Free Masons, you would get into heaven.

On May 15, 2004, I received a phone call from my dad's wife, Maxine. Dad had recently become sick and after seeing a doctor, my dad was diagnosed with lung and bone cancer. They gave him five or six months to live. This was the time of year that I was preparing for my summer camps, but even so, my wife and I made plans to fly to San Francisco as soon as we could get away.

On May 31, we walked into my dad's house again. This time, instead of him greeting us at the door, Maxine greeted us and led us to his bedroom where he lay

asleep, due to all of the pain medication he was taking.

I knew that we didn't have long to spend in San Francisco; I left immediately following our summer staff's boot camp. Camp was going to be starting in just a few days, but I had to have the opportunity to see my father. So the next day, June 1, my wife and I left our hotel room to see him one more time. This time he was awake.

Dad developed an appetite and was craving mashed potatoes, so my wife and I picked up some Kentucky Fried Chicken. As we all sat at the kitchen table, I had the opportunity to pray with my dad for the first time as we blessed our food. As we ate, I noticed dad was wearing a pair of shorts and no shirt, a trait that he obviously passed on to me, as I like to eat like that as well. The similarities I found between us, despite the fact that I never really knew him, amazed me. I began to think of all of the qualities I may have gotten from my dad that I haven't even noticed yet.

It was at that moment that I asked Maxine, "Maxine, if you were to die today, would you go to heaven?"

She proceeded to tell me about her salvation in the fourth grade and explained to me how my being in their lives made her think about how she was living and that she needed to be back in church.

I then asked my father, "Dad, if you were to die today, would you go to heaven?" His comment shocked

me.

"I've been a bastard all my life. That is how I've lived, and that's how I'm going to die."

I immediately thought of John 8 where Jesus was referred to as a bastard, which means illegitimate, and I told my dad that it was interesting that he would compare himself to Jesus. I could tell he began to think, and I explained to him that all of us had been that or worse.

He replied, "But I didn't want to come to God like this, on my death bed, at the last minute."

I dropped the subject momentarily, and we finished eating and took Dad back to his bedroom to lie down. He looked sick and miserable, and I asked him if I could pray with him. He agreed, and by the time the prayer was over Maxine, my wife, and I were all crying.

"Dad, do you believe Jesus loves you, that He died for you, and that He rose from the dead?" I began to share the gospel with him.

"I believe all of that," he said.

"Do you believe it enough to ask Him to save you?" I asked.

Again he replied, "Well, I just didn't want to do it like this."

"I know you didn't want to, but if you believe it, Jesus can save you. Here's what I'm going to do. I need you to understand that a prayer is not what saves you; it's only what you believe in your heart, but I'm going to pray. If you want to ask Christ to save you today, then you repeat after me. If you don't, then I'll finish praying, and it will be done."

As I began to pray, "Dear Lord," though it was only seconds, it seemed like eternity before I heard my father's voice follow coarsely after mine. As we finished praying and Dad looked up he said, "I've never had this much peace in my life."

"Do you believe that He saved you?" I asked.

"Yes."

We visited just a short time more, and my wife and I began to get ready to leave. Suddenly, my dad grabbed me and pulled me toward him, "Don't go," he said. The words were like a foreign language to me. I never thought my dad would ask me not to go.

"I bet you would have been a great son," he whispered in my ear.

"I know you would have been a great dad," I replied.

As he slipped off to sleep that day I sensed the glory of God in his room. Though I was deep in the midst of my annual Wild Week camps, I still tried to call my dad a few times after our visit, but the medicine had him sleeping away most of what was left of his life. Maxine kept us updated on his condition, and one day, twelve days after our leaving San Francisco, I received a call from her.

I'll never forget that day. We were hosting the

camp for the first week of a two-week stop in Columbus, Texas. There was just a short period of time before I had to preach, and Maxine's news made it only harder for me that night. Maxine told me that Jim, my father, woke up from a nap and told her that he saw Jesus standing in the room. He told her that he thought he would fall back asleep and not wake up again.

Believing he was probably hallucinating, she gave him some more morphine for the pain, and he went peacefully back to sleep. My dad was right. He never woke up. At seventy-eight years old, my dad missed hell by twelve days. Among Thorns led us into the presence of God that night at Columbus, Texas, and I looked out at the 1,000 students that were there. I knew momentarily I was going to present a message to these students under conditions that I've never had to deal with before. As the auditorium was still fairly dark, with the exception of the stage lighting, and the keyboard played lightly behind me, I told the students and adults at camp that night about the event that just happened in my life. Many had heard my story. Many had not. So I briefly summarized the relationship that my dad and I had up until just a few years prior. I told of the many years that we had no contact at all, and I told about our joyous reunion. This time, however, I had the incredible news that my dad had accepted Christ, and that as I stood there at that moment, my dad was standing with Jesus.

In the midst of my story, a youth leader from the audience came hurriedly to the stage. He was a bigger guy, and my first thought was that he wanted to fight me, but instead he approached me weeping.

"Brother Ken, I don't mean to interrupt, but I need to forgive my dad. I hate him," he could barely get the words out. I assured him that he wasn't an interruption, and I recognized that God had completely taken over the service.

"Are there any more of you out there who really just need to forgive a dad, a mom, or a family member?" I hadn't even finished the question, and there was a flood of people at the front of the auditorium. What I initially thought was going to be an interruption, God immediately turned into an invitation. I didn't even preach that night, but it was by far the best night at camp we had that summer. God's presence was evident, and we had over one hundred decisions made for Christ that night, over eighty were for salvation.

It's funny; the decisions that were made that night had nothing to do with my testimony. Those decisions were made as a result of my dad's testimony. Though he had only been saved for twelve days, God gave my dad an incredible testimony. In fact, death itself couldn't stop my dad's testimony from spreading. I include my dad's testimony every time I preach my own. Right now as you're reading this book, you are hearing my dad's testimony. It's amazing that God can use the testimony of a man who became a Christian twelve days before his death. Not to mention the fact that during those twelve days he didn't leave his home, but was forced to sleep the majority of the time. He didn't go do great things, he didn't yell about his salvation from the rooftops, but God works despite our circumstances. So, if God can use my dad's testimony to advance his kingdom, what does He want to do with yours? God has a purpose for all of our lives. In fact, He has a plan for all of your life. Are you in line with what God has planned for your life? Is your testimony speaking as loudly as my deceased father's? If it's not, what do you need to do to change that? If God can use a dead man's testimony to lead others to Him, you better believe he can use yours!

## DEVO

Is there someone in your life who still hasn't accepted Christ that you have witnessed to and/or shared your testimony with?

How could you share your testimony with this person through your actions rather than just your words?

Read Daniel 6:1–5 and Titus 2:7–8.

I've heard some say that we are the only Bible some people read. There is truth in that statement. Thinking back to before I was saved, I can remember watching families walk into church on a Sunday morning. They were typically arguing and bickering, nothing like the love they claimed. If this was Christianity, I wanted nothing to do with it. Unfortunately, their actions were the only Bible I was reading at the time.

Daniel obviously led the kind of life that showed others integrity and honor. In fact, when others sought to find a charge against him, they were forced to create a decree forbidding the act that Daniel was so passionate about, worshiping God. The testimony of Daniel's actions was even stronger than his verbal testimony.

## Challenge

Pick one person to whom you can share the love of Christ. Then, list several ways you can show that person the love of Christ through your actions. Strive to complete half of your list.

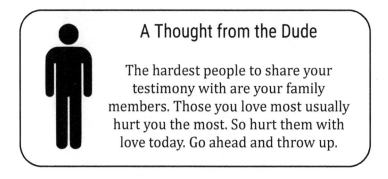

### A Thought from the Dude

The hardest people to share your testimony with are your family members. Those you love most usually hurt you the most. So hurt them with love today. Go ahead and throw up.

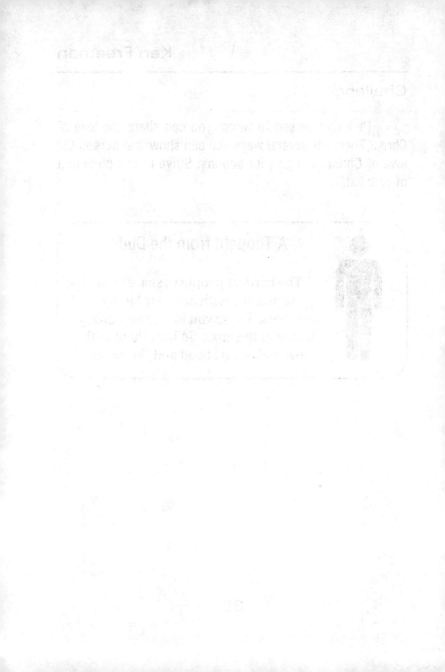

# ONE CHOICE AWAY FROM A DIFFERENT LIFE

When I found my sister Donna in 1998, I was shocked to see that the choices she made had turned her into the very person she hated the most: our mother. The first time I saw her, she appeared to be drunk and stoned; she probably only weighed seventy pounds, and she may have had twelve teeth in her mouth if she was lucky.

Prior to our meeting, Donna had already been diagnosed with Hepatitis C and Cirrhosis of the liver. She had also been in and out of many relationships, just as our mother had, and without the common bond of Jesus in those relationships, they all failed.

Erwin McManus, in his book *Seizing Your Divine Moment*, writes that we are all just one choice away from a different life. This was true for my sister, even in the midst of her dirt and disease. One choice could have saved her from the hell she was living. However, Donna's past choices made her life bitter, not better.

After Donna and I reunited we kept in touch often, which gave me the opportunity to witness to her every chance that I could. My witnessing to her, however, went far beyond verbal communication. In fact, the first thing my family and I did for Donna was send her a $1,000 check to have the rest of her teeth cut out and a set of dentures made for her. I desperately wanted her to have her smile back, and my wife and I believed that this was the first step to building a relationship in which we could share the love of Jesus with her.

The more my sister and I became reacquainted, the more I saw the love Donna held for people. Nothing gave her more joy than to extend a helping hand to another and to really be able to show others that she cared for them. Unfortunately, it seemed as if the people she chose to help were the same people who encouraged Donna to make poor choices. I have always said, "If you show me your friends, I can show you your future." I can accurately say this because I saw the way Donna's friends negatively impacted her life. These friends that she cared so deeply about and was extending a helping hand to were the same friends that were moving their lifestyles, drug addictions, and alcoholism into Donna's life and home. With these influences constantly in her life, the chances of Donna changing her lifestyle were slim.

One night in 2001, I received a terrifying phone call from Donna. As she sat in her vodka-infested, small apartment in the projects of St. Louis, she had come to the conclusion that the only way out of the hell she lived was to kill herself and her biracial son. Living in

San Antonio, I begged Donna to give me twenty-four hours before she made any choices. As I hung up the phone that evening, I had no idea how to help my sister. She wasn't a Christian, but that wasn't a choice that I could make for her. I immediately called a preacher I knew in Bethalto, Illinois, a town not far from where my sister lived in St. Louis. The preacher paid a visit to my sister and her young son early the next day. After some time, the meeting resulted in my sister accepting Jesus Christ as her Savior. Thrilled, I immediately sent my sister and her son Bibles, and since Donna had never received her driver's license, I began contacting various churches closer to her home to take her in. What happened during this time is a sad testimony of where our churches are today.

After contacting several churches in St. Louis, I realized that finding a church that would step into my sister's world of government housing and addiction was going to be much harder than I expected. It really scared me, as the church is supposed to be a hospital for the sick. The church doesn't exist for those who are well, but for those who aren't. Some churches, however, expect individuals to clean themselves up before walking into their sanctuary. Who knows, they may stain the carpet with their vomit. One way or another, many churches I spoke to made the choice to reject my sister.

Finally, several weeks later, I was preaching at a

Wild Week camp in South Carolina, and as I was telling my testimony to the campers, I began to talk about my sister and my discouragement with trying to find a church home for her. I never would have guessed that there were folks from a church in St. Louis, which is approximately fifteen hours from where the camp was held, would be sitting in the congregation that night.

A youth leader approached me after the service ended. He was the youth leader at a new missions-minded church called Have Bible, Will Travel that was constructed quite close to where my sister was living. Pastor Randy and his church were more than glad to visit her and to invite her into their church family.

I had been assisting Donna financially for a long period of time when this church took Donna in as their mission. They often brought her food and clothing, and due to the fact that Donna didn't have a license, they even started a Bible study in her home on Tuesday nights. Though Donna was still struggling with drugs and alcohol, there did seem to be a joy in her life that had not been there prior to this church becoming a part of her life. Donna now had people in her life that genuinely cared about her, and Donna now had genuine people to care about. Donna, too, began to throw up (share her testimony) in her neighborhood.

I thank God for Pastor Randy and his church family. Their church made a choice to visit my sister in the midst of her mess and to show this woman the real love of Jesus Christ. My sister didn't need a Bible dropped on her doorstep; she didn't even need that tract that was sent to her in the mail. My sister needed a church, clothes, food, and love. She needed a family that would love her despite her addictions, despite her friends, despite her lifestyle, despite her neighborhood, despite her past, and that was exactly what this small St. Louis church did for her. They threw up on my sister.

The first time my sister heard me preach I was preaching a revival at First Baptist Church in Ferguson, Missouri in 2003. I'll never forget that evening, as Donna sat on the front row in a black pant suit that she probably bought at a thrift store, or had been given to her by her church family. Donna looked better that night than I had ever seen her look before. As I preached, she cried and took pictures of me. It must have been a roll of thirty-six, because the flash never stopped.

She behaved similarly the second time she heard me preach, which was at the Carlinville, Illinois Wild Week camp in 2004. Pastor Randy brought her that evening, and again, she sat on the front row and cried. After I had finished preaching, I pointed Donna out to the 1,100 people who immediately stood, unprompted, to give Donna a standing ovation. I can tell you assuredly that the love those people showed to her that evening was a defining moment in Donna's life. I had never seen her so happy. I believe this to be one of the rare times in her life where she really felt as if people cared about her. Unfortunately, that was the last time I ever saw Donna.

I received a phone call from Pastor Randy on March 16, 2005. He didn't sound alarmed or upset; in fact, he didn't express much emotion at all at the beginning of our conversation. He asked me to sit down, and he proceeded to tell me about the Bible study they had the night before at Donna's apartment. Pastor Randy talked about Luke 16, the story of the Rich Man and Lazarus. Randy told me of how Donna had been overly excited about verse 22, which reads, "Finally, the beggar died and was carried away by the angels to be with Abraham." Donna was ecstatic about the thought of the angels carrying her away when she died.

After the Bible study ended and everyone left Donna's apartment, Donna made a choice to drink vodka and take pain medication. Donna then went to bed.

Donna's son woke early the next morning and crept quietly out of the house, not wanting to wake her. Another woman and her infant child were living with Donna at the time. The woman had errands to run that morning as well, so she took her baby into Donna's room and laid her gently in bed with her. When Donna's son came home later that night, he found his mother dead. She had been dead for almost twenty-four hours. I believe the angels carried her home.

We don't know for sure whether Donna's death was intentional, but we assume that it probably was. Either way, Donna made a choice, and her choice cost her everything. I still believe she didn't realize that she was one choice away from a different life.

Donna's funeral was to fall on a Monday, a day that I was scheduled to be preaching a revival at a church in Roanoke, Virginia. Being a normal Sunday through Wednesday revival, I requested that the funeral fall in the morning or early afternoon so I could catch a plane to St. Louis for the funeral, and then fly back before I was supposed to preach that evening. Despite my efforts, however, Donna's son (who made the arrangements) made a choice to have the funeral in the evening.

I knew the pastor of the church I was preaching in would have completely understood had I taken the night to go to my sister's funeral. However, I didn't believe it was God's will, nor would it have been what my sister would have wanted me to do. I believe Donna would rather me stay and preach to people just like her, and that's exactly what I did. That evening, my dead sister, who was being put into the ground hundreds of miles away, had a bigger impact on God's kingdom than I did. Her testimony was bright and powerful that night, and more than twenty people chose Christ as their Savior that evening. Many of them related to my sister's struggles.

Bad choices ultimately led to the death of my sister. Again, I don't think she realized that one choice could have led her to a drastically different life. A choice to walk within God's plan for her life would have made all the difference. However, God is continuing to use her testimony, just as he is my dad's.

## DEVO

When my sister chose to live her life like our mother, she made a choice to let her past define her future. Is there any event or mistake in your past that is currently defining your life today?

Realizing this, what choices can you make today to ensure that your past does not define your future?

Read 2 Samuel 11 and Acts 13:22.

Like most of us have, David found himself in several situations that went against God's will for his life. One of these situations included an encounter with Bathsheba, a married woman. This encounter resulted in David lusting over Bathsheba. He then had sex with Bathsheba, and she became pregnant. This sin eventually led to the murder of Bathsheba's husband and the death of the baby. David had to do a lot of scheming and lying to get himself out of the mess he created. However, David didn't allow his past mistakes to define his future. In fact, David even went on to be called "a man after God's own heart." It is important to remember that just like David, God doesn't dwell on our past, and we shouldn't either. Whether it's a mistake you made or circumstances you have no control over, understand that God is ready to use you now, despite your past.

# Toilet Bowl Christianity

## Challenge

Identify an event in your past that had the potential to affect the way you lived in the future. Did you choose to allow that event to define your future, or did you accept it and move on with what God had for your future? Either way, recall times in your life since that event where God has used you or could have used you despite your past. Use these times as encouragement for the future.

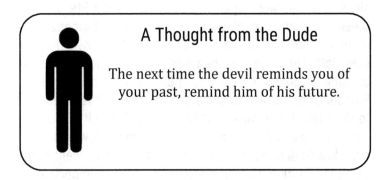

## A Thought from the Dude

The next time the devil reminds you of your past, remind him of his future.

# SMORGASBORD OF CHOICES

I bet as you read this today you have already made many choices. In fact, I bet you have made more choices than you are even aware of. It all started when you got out of bed. Believe it or not, that act alone was a choice. Failing to make the best choice in that situation may have resulted in your being late to school or work, but it was a choice nonetheless. However, the first choice you make today will be your attitude.

After getting out of bed, you had the choice to take a shower, a choice of what to wear, a choice of what to eat for breakfast, a choice to not eat breakfast at all, a choice to apply your Right Guard (and for the sake of others, your left guard, too), and a choice to brush your teeth. You made all of these choices, and that was probably just within your first hour of the day. The truth is we all face and make hundreds of choices daily, and the choices we make have the ability to make us bitter or make us better. You can live this day bummed out or blessed.

It is important to understand when making all of these choices, that God gave you the ability and the privilege to do so. One thing that separates us from other living organisms is our ability to make choices. For example, if a dog wakes up one morning and decides he wants to be a cat, his choice won't matter. He will always be a dog. However, if I woke up this morning and decided that I wanted to be a construction worker, or a waiter, or a singer, I could make that choice. I may not be completely successful at any of those professions, but I could make the choice to pursue them. You were created with the power to choose.

However, part of God's gift of choice is the ability to discern between choices that are within God's will for our lives and those that are not. Take Adam and Eve, for example. They lived in a world of right choices. In fact, they only had one wrong choice. However, just as we often stray from the good choices to pursue the bad, Adam and Eve walked through all of the right trees to find the wrong one, which was in the center of The Garden. That one choice gave birth to the disease we still fight today, sin. In fact, as punishment for their wrong choice, God says in Genesis 3:17 "Because you listened to your wife and ate the fruit I told you not to eat, I have placed a curse on the ground. All your life you will struggle to scratch a living from it." Your testimony is a choice.

Ironically enough, in Chapter 4 of Genesis when Cain and Abel presented their offerings to God, God did not accept Cain's offering, which just happened to come from the ground that God previously cursed. The story concludes with Cain murdering his brother, Abel, because God accepted his offering, and this made Cain angry and jealous. Cain made a choice. He chose to be drunk with jealousy.

Just as the one choice that Adam and Eve made affected many people and resulted in bitter consequences, our choices can have the same effect. For example, one choice to go to one party can cost a person everything. Maybe it's a car accident on the way home, maybe it's being raped, or maybe it's losing the trust of your parents. Regardless, circumstances would leave us saying, "It could have been different."

In reality, our choices, whether bad or good, affect more than we realize. Just as the sin of Adam and Eve affected their children and is still affecting us today, our choices can also affect our families, friends, future, and fellowship with God. Romans 5:12 says that because of one man, Adam (his choice to make the bad choice), sin has infected the whole world. There is power in one choice. Judas' choice to betray Jesus very much affected his future, as he made a choice to hang himself. The choice of the disciples to go to sleep after Jesus asked them to pray, affected their fellowship with God, just as some choices we make can separate us from God and some can bring us nearer to Him.

We humans aren't the only ones who make choices. In fact, the Bible tells us that God Himself makes choices. The choice He made was you. Me. Sinners. God's choice was for us to be His children. James 1:18 says: "In his goodness he chose to make us his own children by giving us his true word. And we, out of all creation, became his choice possession."

Of all the choices God could have made, He chose us. Because of the kindness of God to choose us, we should choose God in all the decisions we make.

Am I going to that party? Choose God.

Should I give attitude to my parents? Choose God.

Should I tithe at church this week? Choose God.

By doing so, we find ourselves in the midst of exactly where God wants us to be. It's at that place that He can use us most effectively.

I do think it is important to mention that making good choices is not always saying "no" to things, but it's about saying "yes" to life. Life is a choice. There were many things I should have said "no" to when I was growing up, but it was not until my salvation and saying "yes" to life that my life really began to reflect God's will for me. It was after this that I had to choose to quit smoking, and I had to choose to forgive my dad. Without first choosing life, I would have had no desire or purpose to make these other choices.

Many years ago when I served as a youth pastor, I had a young girl in my youth group named Beth. At seventeen, Beth accepted Jesus Christ as her Savior and chose life for the first time. Years later, both she and her sister married and had children. Without warning, Beth's nephew became ill and was admitted to a local hospital. Days passed and doctors remained baffled at the boy's illness. The boy died just days later. Within less than a week, Beth's other nephew, her sister's only remaining child, became ill with the same disease and died as well. Two children, two sons, two nephews, two grandchildren, all gone within a week's time. This will forever be a part of their parents' testimony.

Not even a year later, Beth sent her daughter Shelby to a church camp. One day while at camp, Shelby complained of a stomach ache and went back to her cabin to lie down. She was found hours later slumped on the floor of her cabin. Shelby died of a massive heart attack at the age of eight. This will forever be Shelby's testimony.

I spoke to Beth on the phone in the midst of the tragedy, and I distinctly remember one comment of Beth's. Through broken speech and tears I heard, "I'm not going to stop loving Jesus. I'm not going to stop loving Jesus." Beth and her husband made a choice. In a desperate time when it would have been incredibly easy to blame God or become angry, Beth chose life. She made a choice that ultimately made her life better, rather than bitter, and offered hope to others dealing with similar situations.

Another quote from Erwin McManus says, "We can't choose how we're going to die, but we can choose how we're going to live." Beth chose to live. Will you?

You wonder why I would include this chapter. We are in a war, and in this war there is going to be hurt, tragedy, and terrorism. In it, we must choose to share our testimony and live our testimony. That's how we win the war (Revelation 12:11).

## DEVO

Are the choices you are currently making bringing you closer to God and making your life better or taking your attention off of God and making your life bitter?

If you've been making decisions that have put distance between you and God, what choices can you make now that will begin to shorten that distance?

Read Romans 6:16, Isaiah 1:18, and Romans 11:11.

It can often be hard, when finding ourselves in the midst of sin, to make choices that will get us out of it. After all, it's often easier to sin with the world than it is to remain faithful to God. However, God tells us in Romans 6:16 that if we choose sin, eventually sin will control us.

Have you ever noticed that the first time you give in to a temptation you feel rather guilty about it, but you think, "Well, I've done it once. I've already messed up. I may as well do it again." Then, after you mess up and mess up and mess up, suddenly you don't feel so guilty about your sin anymore? This is because your sin is becoming your master. Suddenly, the guilt goes away because God isn't the ruler of your life anymore. As the guilt goes away, you feel even more comfortable to go on sinning. This is a very dangerous place for a Christian to be.

However, light shines to those of us who have found ourselves in that situation in Isaiah 1:18 and Romans 11:11. Isaiah 1:18 reads, "No matter how deep the stain of your sins, I can remove it. I can make you as clean as freshly fallen snow. Even if you are stained as red as crimson, I can make you as white as wool." Romans 11:11a reads, "Did God's people stumble and fall beyond recovery? Of course not!"

These verses show that we can't believe Satan's lie that says, "You've already done it once. There's no being pure for you. God won't forgive you this time." God chooses to forgive us, according to 1 John 1:9. If we confess our sins, our wrong choices, to God, He will forgive us and cleanse us of all unrighteousness. That is a promise. So if today there is guilt, there's shame, there's blame, you feel like you're being accused, the devil has chosen to attack you with this, will you believe the lie of the devil or trust the truth of God? It's your choice to be bummed out and bitter or blessed and better.

## Challenge

You can't get closer to God than you are right now because if you're a Christian, He's in you. But you can become stronger in God. What steps will you take today to become stronger in your faith with God and your fellowship with God's people? Make it a choice to hang with people who make godly choices. Make a list of who those people are and surround yourself with them. Spend time in God's Word. Take Proverbs, thirty-one chapters, and for the next month read a chapter a day. Be faithful to your church. Here's the key—live your convictions, be strong with your commitments, and always be consistent. What actions do you need to take today to shorten the distance between you and the God who loves you?

## A Thought from the Dude

You can make thousands upon thousands of right choices every day, but it only takes one wrong choice to nullify all of the right ones.

# TOILET BOWL TESTIMONIES

So what do all of our choices have to do with our testimonies? Everything! Not only do the choices we make affect our testimonies, but we also make many choices regarding whether or not we share our testimonies.

When I look into the lives of my family, it is obvious to see how the choices made affected our life stories. My mother made choices that resulted in hate, anger, depression, and disease. My sister made a choice to ultimately live like our mother, but she did eventually choose life, which brought her the only real happiness she ever experienced. My dad chose to not be a part of our family for decades, and when he finally chose life, he didn't have much time to enjoy it. I, on the other hand, made a choice that would forever affect my friends, my family, and my eternity, and I'm still making those choices today.

You see, the choices that we make have the ability to make our testimonies stronger or the ability to make our testimonies weaker. Judas made a choice. He wanted power and popularity. All of us are bombarded, both young and old, adults, teenagers, and children, for power and popularity. Judas chose to hang with the wrong crowd, and that choice hung him. Peter also made a choice, whether because of embarrassment or fear, to deny Jesus, not once, but three times. The crowd asked him, "Weren't you the one with Jesus?" Peter made a choice. The difference between Judas and Peter, one hung himself, and the other fell at the feet that hung for him. Peter was used by God because he made the right choice. Live loud and throw up hard for Jesus.

Many people believe wrongly that our testimony stops when we get baptized, join the church, or walk an aisle. Your testimony doesn't begin with any of these things. Those are all good and right things, but your testimony begins with your personal relationship with Jesus Christ. If you're listening say, "I AM." Did you hear what I said? That is where it begins, but it doesn't end there. From that moment on, your testimony continues to grow and take shape as you, as a Christian, strive to become more and more like Christ.

So why does the church insist that we share our testimonies? Because we hold the one true story that no one can argue. For centuries, people have been looking for error in the Bible, and they continue to argue God's word. However, as much as they want to argue what's recorded in black and white, they can't argue the change that's happened in your life. They can't argue the flesh and blood that stands before them as a witness to what Christ has done. Having a testimony calls you to be a witness for Christ, just as having a testimony in a court case would make you a witness in a trial. Unfortunately, Christ's witnesses aren't taking the stand. They aren't sharing. Why? I believe there are several main reasons why a Christian doesn't share his or her testimony.

First, you may not have a testimony. It's impossible to share the effect that Christ has had on your life if you've never invited Him into your life. I challenge you, if you call yourself a Christian yet firmly believe you don't have a testimony, to really evaluate your salvation experience. You may not be a Christian. Understand that God does want to do things in your life, and all you have to do is invite him to do those things and make him Lord over your life and your choices.

A second reason is that many people don't know how to share their testimony. It isn't that you don't have one, but suddenly when the conversation turns to your faith, you freeze. I remember the first time I shared my testimony; I was nineteen and was in Midland, Texas. My wife and I still listen to the tape sometimes, and it is amazing to hear the difference in my confidence, my tone of voice, and even my vocabulary. Sharing our testimony with others is just as easy as sharing the story about how your team won the game yesterday. (Go, Cowboys, Go!) It is a familiar story to you that can be shared with others. I know about a lot of things:

sports, movies, actors, politics, television, etc., and I use all of these things to my advantage, trying to figure out how I'm going to get Jesus into my conversation. So if you want to know how to share your faith, hang around people who share their faith.

Fear is also a reason that people don't share. In fact, this may be the biggest reason. Talking about the game yesterday makes for easy conversation, but now you've been asked why you are going to church tomorrow instead of golfing with the guys. You have the perfect opportunity to share with them your love for Jesus and all of the wonderful things he has done in your life, but suddenly you freeze. You've forgotten everything. "What do I do?" you panic. "What are they going to think of me?" So rather than tell them about the love of Jesus and about the incredible thing he did in your life last week, you quickly mumble, "I've gotta be at church. The wife's making me." And you quickly change the subject back to yesterday's game. Opportunity lost. Crisis averted.

Are you afraid people will find out that you are a Christian? You shouldn't be, because people should already know that you are a Christian by the way you act. You should stand out from the world.

Maybe you are afraid of persecution. Don't be afraid of that either. The Bible says that we will be persecuted (Matthew 5). It's a certainty. So don't be scared of it. Welcome it. Christ was persecuted, and we will be as well. The Bible says when people make fun of you or cast insults at you, it's really not at you; it is at the Jesus in you. Matthew 5 says to have a party when you're persecuted for Jesus. If you're going to throw up (share your testimony), get a party whistle, and the next time you are made fun of, blow it. They may never come around you again, but the point is proven. Your testimony is a party, share it.

Fear of failure is another reason people don't share. It isn't the rejection or the persecution, they are simply afraid of failing in their attempts to tell someone about Jesus. The only time we fail is when we fail to tell. It is only when we pass up opportunities that we become failures. It doesn't matter if the person you've shared with acccepts Christ due to your testimony or if they shrug it off. You have still done your part, and that is all you can do. If they have just shrugged off your efforts, know that a seed has been planted in their hearts. 1 Corinthians 3:6–9 says, "My job was to plant the seed in your hearts, it's another person to water, but God who makes it grow." It takes a team to win people to Jesus. Start planting in your garden today. "Where is my garden?" you ask. Your garden is where you live; your home, your school, your job, your squad, your friends, your team, your life. Grow a garden for God. Throw up today in your garden. (Fertilizer, right?)

The last reason I believe some people choose not to share is probably the scariest, and I keep finding this more and more in the church today. Apathy. Some people just really don't care. They sit in their pew on Sunday, say the "Oh Jesus" and "Amen" at the directed times, and go about their life, not really caring that everyone who is around them is lost and going to hell. That is apathy. They make a choice not to share their testimony simply because they really don't see the point. This is the most dangerous reason for not sharing your testimony. If you find yourself in this position, you should research your heart and evaluate your salvation. One characteristic of a Christian is a heart that cares about the salvation and damnation of others and a heart that longs to advance God's kingdom. In Luke 10 the question was asked, "Who is my neighbor?" Jesus then shared the story about the Good Samaritan, the preacher, and the church member. All three saw the same man lying on the side of the road, half dead. The preacher and the church member had just left church and walked to the other side of the road, because they didn't care and didn't want to get involved. The Samaritan, the outcast, the one who didn't fit in, is the one who shared his life with someone he didn't even know. So Jesus asked the question, "Who do you think showed mercy?" The religious man answered, "It's the one that did something." You need to pray for a heart that believes in heaven and believes in hell. Final answer... do something today. Throw up on somebody. If you aren't sharing your testimony, you can probably place yourself in one of the categories above. Maybe you don't have a testimony, maybe you don't know how, maybe you are afraid, or maybe you are apathetic.

Whichever category you may place yourself in, there are ways to overcome your excuse for not sharing.

For those of you who don't have a testimony, get one. You have the simplest solution of all of these. How do you get one? Evaluate your salvation. If you come to the conclusion that you've never fully given up your life to Christ, do that. Make him Lord over your life, and you have a testimony. Those who are apathetic may start at the same position. Evaluate your salvation. If you truly believe you are a Christian, evaluate your life, because there may be sin that is keeping God from hearing you. (Isaiah 59:2 says, "But there is a problem—your sins have cut you off from God. Because of your sin, he has turned away and will not hear anymore.") In this case, you need to weed the sin out of your life. At that point, God may begin working in your life in incredible ways.

For the people who simply don't know how to share your testimony, practice it. You know in your heart exactly what God has done in your life, all you have to be able to do is put it into words. Your testimony shouldn't be so rehearsed that it sounds rehearsed. Instead, just look for opportunities to share. Just like in the scenario before, the man was completely set up by his friends to share his testimony. He had the perfect opportunity to just say, "Guys, God has just done some awesome things in my life, and I'm really looking forward to going to church tomorrow to thank Him for them." That sentence alone is a testimony. After that statement you may be asked what God has done in your life that is so great. Suddenly, you haven't forced your testimony onto anyone, and it's flowing very well with conversation.

If you're afraid, realize again that if you are really living a life that is glorifying to God, people already know that you are a Christian, and eventually you will be persecuted to some degree because of your Christianity. Realize this, you do not have all of the answers, but don't ever forget that you have the only answer that matters, Jesus. God's Word offers hope through this persecution. 2 Thessalonians 1:5–7a says God will use this persecution to show His justice. For He will make you worthy of his Kingdom, for which you are suffering, and in His justice He will punish those who persecute you. And God will provide rest for you who are being persecuted.

Don't be afraid to fail. Again, we can never fail when sharing our testimonies. Some of the greatest people in the world were failures. Einstein. Edison. Beethoven. Michael Jordan failed to make his junior high basketball team. How would you have liked to have been the coach to cut him? Failing for the faith is not failing.

Through Hurricane Rita and Hurricane Katrina I

believe we all saw an outstanding display of the testimony of the church. In disaster relief efforts it wasn't FEMA or the American Red Cross that were standouts. (Don't misunderstand me; these people did hold a part in relief efforts.) However, it was the church that stood out. It was the church who took people in and fed them when they had nowhere to go. It was youth leaders and pastors whose churches had been demolished who weren't working to rebuild their own church, but instead they were all working together, rescuing those still trapped by the storm, feeding the homeless, and working with chainsaws and hammers to begin cleaning up the hurricane-ravished area. It was the church who opened up support groups for families who had lost loved ones. It was the church who extended open arms and provided a facility to teach students who had lost their school buildings. Did the church do these things to be recognized? No. The church took part because they held a real love for people that went far beyond praying for those affected, and instead, became an answer to prayer. Because of this, the testimony of the church has shone brightly enough for people all over the country to ask, "Why? What exactly is it that they have that makes them different?" That alone is a testimony. They threw up, now it's your turn.

## DEVO

What excuses are you using for not sharing your testimony?

What can you do personally to eliminate these excuses from your life?

Read Acts 20:24–27 and Acts 22:15.

God has put us on this earth for one reason and one reason only, to give Him glory. One way that we give God glory is by sharing the story He has given us with others.

Paul tells us in Acts that our lives are worth nothing unless we use them for declaring the Good News of God's love. That seems like a very strong statement, but that is exactly what God's Word tells us in Acts 20:24. That means that our jobs, our education, and our families are all worth nothing if we don't use them to spread the word about Jesus. Have you ever thought of your job as a mission field? If not, it's time to start.

You aren't here to become rich or successful, but you are here to make God famous. That is your only job. You don't go to the bank to cash a check, you go to throw up (share your testimony). But while you're there, cash the check. You don't go to school for an education, I know the students love that statement. You go to school (cafeteria) to throw up, but while you're there, get an education. You don't go to work to go to work; you go to work to throw up, but while you're there make a living. Your testimony is not an option, it's an obligation to share.

## Challenge

Who are the hardest people to throw up on (share Jesus with) today? Write their names down, pray for them daily, and ask God to give you opportunities to share your testimony. Remember, your mission field is where you live. You can't win the people around you by yourself. Get a partner that will work with you and pray with you to win friends and family to Jesus. I make this challenge, find one person a week for the next four weeks and pray for that one person for seven days. On the seventh day, witness to them. Remember, you are planting seeds and watering. God will grow it.

### A Thought from the Dude

If your friends were the jury in a courtroom and you were on trial because of your testimony for Jesus, would your lost friends declare you guilty or not guilty of being a Christian?

# IF YOU ARE LISTENING, SAY, "I AM!"

In Exodus 3, a shepherd and murderer named Moses comes into contact witih God for the first time by way of a burning bush. During this meeting, God informs Moses that he is the vessel God wants to use to rescue His people from the Egyptians. After some debate, Moses surrenders himself to God's plan, but has one remaining question, "If I go to the people of Israel and tell them, 'The God of your ancestors has sent me to you,' they won't believe me. They will ask, 'Which god are you talking about? What is his name?' Then what should I tell them?"

God responds simply, "I am the one who always is. Just tell them, 'I AM has sent me to you.'" Moses heard God's response and followed through with God's request. Moses ultimately led God's people to the Promised Land because he truly listened to what God had to say.

Anyone who has heard me preach has heard me use a line that has caught on through the years: If you're listening say, "I am." I've always used this method to keep people's attention throughout my messages.

However, as time has gone on, the catch phrase has taken on more and more meaning.

I AM is just one of the incredible names by which we know God. His name is all-encompassing and powerful. There is strength and might in the name I AM. When I use the line, "If you're listening say, 'I am,'" I can't help but believe that God is saying the same thing.

God is longing for us, like Moses, to listen to Him, to hear His voice, to feel His touch, and to say His name. In our success-driven culture, however, time is just one of the many evils God has to battle to get us to pay attention. He simply wants us to listen to His voice and respond to Him. Listening to God is vital to having a relationship with Him. You can't have a relationship with someone to whom you've never spoken or listened to. It is simply impossible.

Without hearing God and really listening to His voice, you have no accurate means on which to base your choices. God is the only one who can lead us and direct our paths, so the choices we face in life lie directly on the shoulders of the Great I AM. He must make our choices for us, because from our choices root our testimonies; and our testimonies lead others to him.

Despite your testimony and the past choices you've made, God is ready, willing, and waiting for you to talk to Him. He wants you to not only hear, but listen to His guidance. He wants you to respond to Him. When

He asks if you're listening, say His name, "I AM." Follow through with the instructions He gives you. He is the author of your life, and He knows exactly where He could use you most effectively, so keep pushing hard after Him, and He will never let you fall.

Exodus 3:14: God said I AM the one who always is.

John 4:26: Then Jesus told her, I AM the Messiah.

John 6:35: Jesus replied, "I AM the bread of life.
No one who comes to Me will ever be hungry again. Those who believe in Me will never thirst."

John 8:12: Jesus said to the people, "I AM the light of the world. If you follow me, you won't be stumbling through the darkness, because you will have the light that leads to life."

John 10:7b: "I assure you I AM the gate for the sheep," he said.

John 10:11: "I AM the good shepherd. Th e good shepherd lays down his life for his sheep."

John 11:25: Jesus told her, "I AM the resurrection and the life. Those who believe in me, even though they die like everyone else, will live again."

John 14:6: Jesus told him, "I AM the way, the truth, the life. No one can come to the Father except through me."

John 15:1: "I AM the true vine, and my Father is the gardener."

I AM is a personal name of God; it's the title or saying by which Jesus identified himself. In John 8, they blasted Jesus because of his testimony. They said he was demon possessed. They said He was suicidal. They said He was illegitimate. They thought he was crazy in John 8:54–58 when He said, "Before Abraham was, I AM."

Maybe like Ken Freeman, you, too, were born out of wedlock, the world may call you illegitimate, but I have good news. You are very legitimate in God's eyes. MC Hammer, before his ministry, put out a song called "Too Legit To Quit." Today, he preaches the gospel of Jesus. If you're going to throw up (share your testimony), make sure you have all of the I AM in your life, so when someone says to you, "What is different about your life?" you have two words, "I AM."

## DEVO

What is keeping you from, not only hearing God, but listening to God today? Is it business? Is it a boyfriend or girlfriend? Is it laziness? Eliminate these distractions, listen to God, and I promise you that you'll hear him. John 10:3 says, "My sheep hear his voice."

This week, write down the times you actually hear from God, like I did in Florida. Where were you? What were you doing? Who were you with? If you have never journaled, this would be a good time to start. I've probably written twenty journals, and I will go back and reflect on the times that I've listened and heard God. Here is how you can hear God: listen when you worship, listen when the word is preached, and listen as he speaks to his creation. God is speaking, and it's not that we don't hear or aren't listening; it's a Christmas song, "Do you hear what I hear?" Start making listening a practice. Practice doesn't make perfect; practice makes permanent.

Read John 12:23–26.

## Challenge

Today, deny yourself. Lose sight of what you want, what you think you need, and take hold of what He wants. Take up your cross. Carry your responsibility, your burdens for lost sheep, hurting sheep, and confused sheep. That includes your friends and your family, and maybe even a stranger. Follow Him daily. Daily means moment by moment, step by step. He said His servants must follow Him, and they will be where I AM. Find out where I AM is, and join Him. John 10 says that God's sheep have three qualities. They hear God, know God, and follow God. Practice these things and you'll hear Him. If you're listening, say, "I AM."

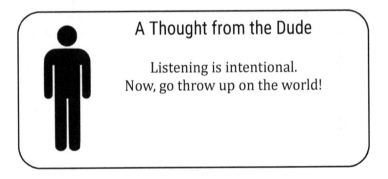

## A Thought from the Dude

Listening is intentional.
Now, go throw up on the world!

# About the Author

With the ability to connect to people of any age group, culture, or background, evangelist Ken Freeman lives with a passion to bring people to know Christ and to make a deeper, more intimate commitment to Him.

Ken has been blessed with a beautiful wife, Debbie, two sons, and ten beautiful grandchildren. He has a grandchild, Trey, who is in Heaven following a battle with cancer that took his young life. His son and daughter-in-law then adopted two babies who were born to a drug-addicted mother. As he says, "One woman's trash became our treasures."

He has a passion for his ministry and he's had an enormous amount of opportunities in the United States and internationally to do what he loves most; lead people to Christ. In his ministry, God has allowed Ken to speak in more than 7,000 churches and in more than 25,000 school assemblies.

Connect with Ken:
www.kenfreeman.com
www.Choices101.com
www.wildweek.com
Instagram: @kdaddyfree
Twitter: @kdaddyfree
www.Facebook.com/kdaddyfree

# Also by Ken Freeman

## CHOICES 101

ISBN: 978-1-942508-36-6

People make choices, and choices make people. Did you know that every day you make choices that affect four major areas of your life? In *Choices 101,* author and evangelist Ken Freeman shares how your daily choices affect your family, your friends, your future, and your faith.

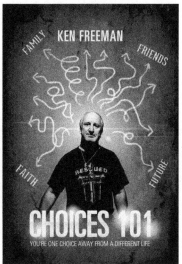

**Available through Ken's website, through Amazon, Barnes and Noble, or order through your local book retailer!**